"*Beyond Haiku* by Captain Linda Pauwels is an amazing sel[...] short poems written by pilots with artwork from their children. It is a quick insightful read containing 51 haikus, 20 short poems and seven pieces of philosophical prose. Her book eloquently describes how pilots are a rare breed that live at the edge of so many continuums: speed, altitude, time, distance, danger, performance, proficiency and emotion. They have unique lives, experiences and perspectives that few of us will ever know. Haikus are an instantaneous snapshot revealing what a pilot was experiencing or thinking about. It's a means to transcend their unique perspective to inspire yours. Captain Pauwels has done an outstanding job organizing and categorizing these snippets for your perusal. The collection is broad to cover the gambit of aviation allowing you to select a topic and deep dive into your own reflections! Pilots are away from their family for long durations so please pay special attention to their children's artwork. Like haikus, their simplistic art style deeply expresses innocent heartfelt messages."

– **Helmut H. Reda**, Editor, *Because I Fly, the world's largest collection of aviation poetry*

"*In Beyond Haiku: Pilots Write Poetry*, American Airlines Captain Linda Pauwels showcases a collection of work penned by fellow pilots, both active and retired. The sections range from deeply reflective verses to short witty haiku, each contributor offering a glimpse into a pilot's life. From the vivid image of a bird in flight to a father longing to see his kids, each poem takes you into the heart and minds of those good folks who've dedicated their careers to getting passengers safely from one place to another.

I highly recommend this book to anyone who's ever traveled through the air, whether you're up front at the controls or buckled into your seatbelt in back on your way from here to there."

– **Kathleen M. Rodgers**, Aviation poet and author of the new novel, *The Flying Cutterbucks.*

FIG
FACTOR
MEDIA

ISBN: 978-1-952779-56-5
Library of Congress Control Number: 2020922665

BEYOND HAIKU:
PILOTS WRITE POETRY

CAPTAIN LINDA PAUWELS

DEDICATION

To all the little boys and girls who grew up to be pilots.

verba volant, scripta manent

TABLE OF CONTENTS:

FOREWORD

William Faulkner is credited with the truism, "Every novelist is a failed short story writer, and every short story writer a failed poet." The truth in these words is less a criticism of fiction writing than it is high praise of the poetic form: poesis is the distillation of life into symbolic, habitable melody. It's thought with motion, spirit with heart, action with direction.

It's no coincidence that those descriptors apply to flying, nor is it happenstance that pilots who live that reality in the air also navigate the ultimate poetic flight on paper. And so, this collection. What could be more apt than the spare but knife-edge slice of Haiku as the medium of pilot-speak in poesis? Where else could those on the ground see through the eyes of the footless and live the truth of life as poetic flight?

In this collection, you'll find wit, grit, soul, and heart. You'll live fire and ice and the pain of leaving; the marshaling of strength and the lament of loss; shiny newness and numbing familiarity. And it's not so much about flying as it is in itself flight, poetic flight.

Sit down, strap in, and enjoy the ride.

-*Chris Manno*, Ph.D., Rhetoric and Literature; Adjunct Professor, Texas Christian University, Fort Worth, TX

American Airlines Captain-retired

ACKNOWLEDGEMENTS

Semper Fi Patrick Clark. Thank you for listening and for believing in this idea early on. Mil gracias, Jackie Ruiz, for sprinkling your pixie dust onto this little book.

To my warrior princess, Nathalie: switching majors to English at USNA turned out to be an inspired decision. Who knew you'd become a valuable sounding board when momma waxed poetic? Be like water.

With sincerest gratitude to my fellow pilots for entrusting me with their words. They will indeed remain when we have flown West.

To our young artists, the beauty of your work is what gives these pages fullness. Thank you, and your parents, for sharing these joyful efforts with us all.

INTRODUCTION

Airline pilots live in a world of structure. We fly by the rules. We read checklists and follow procedures. We use models that teach us about trapping errors and managing threats. And because our thinking style is generally concrete and practical, we learn how to compartmentalize in order to fly safely and keep the blue side up.

Beyond Haiku deconstructs some of that rigidity. It allows those on the other side of the cockpit door- passengers, colleagues, and even family members- a glimpse of emotions that pilots, typically viewed as cool and distant, wryly 'put into a box' to perform calmly and with clarity. There is a softer side to the men and women who fly, though it can easily get buried in the daily rigors of the job. Perhaps this is the greatest misnomer Beyond Haiku fulfills. It gives pilots themselves latitude to grieve, to suffer, to love, to feel loss… and to write about it, as poets have done for millennia.

The selections featured in this book are by active, retired, furloughed, medically disabled, and deceased pilots. The majority were curated from two poetry threads residing on an internal discussion forum called The Line, hosted by the Allied Pilots Association. A few were sent to me directly. Some that I penned myself have not been shared until now. The selections are grouped into six themes: 1) On Haiku; 2) On Flying; 3) On Nature and Beauty; 4) Vignettes of a Pilot's Life; and 5) On Love, Hearth, and Home. The final theme, 6) On Continuity, contains compositions by pilots undergoing flight training through the American Airlines Cadet Academy.

Five years ago, I started the first thread, titled *Morning Haiku*. It was an unusual idea, as poetry is not known to be popular among mostly male aviators. However, my more than three decades of experience as an airline pilot, combined with an academic background in education and the study of job stress and stress resilience, suggested poetry might provide benefits to the group. When we modernized platforms, the thread became *Beyond Haiku*. In addition to original poems, all types of poetry and quotations were posted on these threads.

The illustrations in the book are by children of pilots, aged 6 to 17. This was a process in itself. First, a request for young artists was posted on the forum. Within hours, several volunteers came forward, and the list kept growing, for a total of seventeen. The artists were asked to send in a sample of their work. Then, based on perception, intuition, and imagination, I selected a poem that would best harmonize with the artist behind the sample and gave each the freedom to create in their own style.

This book is a labor of love. It is by pilots, for the benefit of pilots. It serves to build unity through poetry by means of co-authorship, shared empathy, and shared creative expression. And it invites children and families to participate, building community during the time of COVID-19 and the resultant crisis in the industry.

All proceeds from *Beyond Haiku: Pilots Write Poetry* will go to the Allied Pilots Association Emergency Relief and Scholarship Fund in support of furloughed pilots and their families.

1) On Haiku:

This haiku, by 18th century Japanese poet Tan Taigi, was the original entry on Morning Haiku, the first poetry thread I started on our internal pilot discussion forum. The date was November 25, 2015:

> *"Don't touch my plumtree!"*
>
> *Said my friend, and saying so*
>
> *broke the branch for me.*[1]

The reaction came quickly: "Okay, I bet I'm not the only one who is saying, 'huh'?" This comment was followed by a back and forth about haiku, dislike of poetry, and of course, the rules for haiku. Pilots are big on rules. Because more structure would tend to inhibit the free flow of feelings, my suggestion was simply 'no rules.'

I realized the idea had promise when another pilot asked, somewhat in jest: "are we going to have an all-new haiku every morning?"

---

[1] Peter Beilenson, ed., *Japanese Haiku* (New York: Peter Pauper, 1955), 14, www.sacred-texts.com

New Year's Day.
Had a bowl of Ramen-
Is this Haiku?

-CA Gerardo Lami, MIA (RET)

Two grasshoppers were
Romping in the dew wet grass
Refrigerator

-CA Robert Sproc, DFW

I am first with five
Then seven in the middle --
Five again to end
How to Haiku

-Contributed by FO Roger Mortensen, PHL

–Sorry Linda…
us Marines need pictures
does that mean we are Loku?

-CKA Gregory Hudson, MIA

Just because
you guys write silly 3-line gibberish
doesn't make it haiku?

-CA John Drindak, LAX

Jethroplex morning
I need five more syllables
To make my Haiku

-CA Robert Sproc, DFW

It's zero zero two two
here in the LAX Westin bar
first haiku today

-CA Robert Sproc, DFW

For a dear friend I Haiku
Vow undone this day
Never to return again

-CKA Wendy Young, DFW

This is a haiku
but having only the form
it lacks the essence

-FO Christopher Lemon, LAX

2) ON FLYING

In The Little Prince, aviator Antoine de Saint Exupéry's fox explains what it means to be tamed: "It is an act too often neglected...it means to establish ties."[2]

Much has changed in the four decades since I first soloed, as a young girl of 16, at Opa-Locka airport. In spite of the rapid technological changes, a human being still remains at the controls of an airliner.

The job of piloting is one of apprenticeship. All of us carry elements of other pilots within us.

"You become responsible, forever, for what you have tamed."[3]

---

[2] Antoine de Saint-Exupéry, *The Little Prince*, (New York: Harcourt Brace & Company, 1943), 18.

[3] Saint-Exupéry, The Little Prince, 68.

Look always for the open field
scan outside like your head was on a swivel
at all times be aware of speed
don't forget carburetor heat
when flaring, think pressure not movement
flying lessons from another time
the voice still lingers in memory
like the third reflection of an echo

-CA Konstantin Volodzko, PHL (RET)

Twenty-five west
Keflavik to port
Horizon shows itself once again
Break is over
Shake off the brief night
Need to fashion a sunshade.
Coffee first.

-CA Konstantin Volodzko, PHL (RET)

After a too long day
Halfway through a night approach
To minimums
In blizzard conditions
Buffeted by moderate turbulence
"Better be a great layover hotel"
Says the captain.

-CA Konstantin Volodzko, PHL (RET)

Zihuatanejo (ZIH)

The Captain invited me up front
listas de chequeo en español
y aqui no hay FOQA
flying over the Sierra Madre del Sur
a tight approach, into an orange sun
landed runway 26
first night, no ear plugs needed
to silence the crashing waves
or the noisy Mexican grackles
roosting in the mangroves
sleep comes easy-
soft breezes dampen my thoughts
under the coconut palms

-CKA Linda Pauwels, MIA

Remembering Challenger

thirty years have gone by
in the blink of an eye
a glimpse of a cold Florida morning
youth and promise lost in the sky
a moment of silence
as we taxi out-
bid sheet to bid sheet
fast forward to the future
a look in the mirror this morning
shows my mother's face
thirty years have gone by
in the blink of an eye

-CKA Linda Pauwels, MIA

It worked yesterday,
but it does not work today.
Boeing is like that.

When the Airbus breaks,
we just reset a breaker
and it works again.
Go A Team!

-CA Thomas Hill, DCA

The ONLY time
you are going too fast
is when you are about to hit something!
Me, 1988 - From the left seat of an MD-80

-CA Ronald Hunt, ORD (RET)

There is a whole life
Beyond the 777
On a mountain strip
In the Cessna 180

-CA Loren Banko, DCA (RET)

San Miguel volcano
spewing ash-
runway lights in sight!

-CKA Linda Pauwels, MIA

3) On Nature And Beauty:

Pilots are intimately attuned to the consequences of nature, most especially the adverse effects of weather. But flying through the quiet blackness of night, in the midst of radio silence, one actually feels enveloped by the majesty that surrounds us.

How do we describe the weight of moonlight shining through the cockpit windows during takeoff? Or the pulsations emanating from the green glow of a dancing aurora borealis? Or the liquid gold flowing from a rising sun directly into the heart?

One of the benefits of haiku is that it helps capture the emotion of a moment in time. Little by little, that ability is reinforced, and translates into other areas of functioning.

Childhood memories
Morph watercolors in rain
Makes new life beauty

-CA Carl Battis, DFW

Mountain snowmelt starts
Sunshine water rules the day
Spring renews us all

-CA Carl Battis, DFW

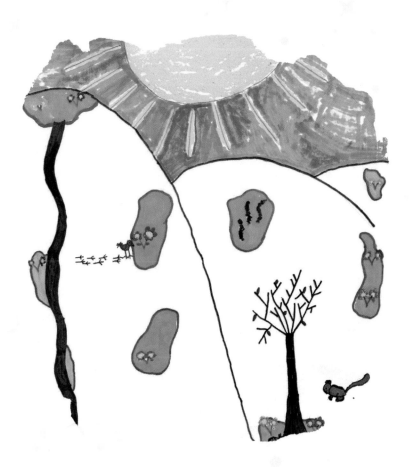

Flying through the night
Waiting for it to happen
Noctilucent clouds

-FO Timothy Hamel, DFW

Soft glow in cockpit
Black sky melts purple then pink
Silently meet the new day

-FO Richard Krutenat, DFW

Fading memories
In the cold winds of Autumn
A pile of dead leaves

-FO Carol Scherer, DFW (RET)

Hues of pink and blue-
sun's parting footprints
grace the firmament

- CKA Linda Pauwels, MIA

17

Sunlight slights its way
Glowing flowers at daybreak
Peering in to say
Good morning!

-CA Mark Treider, DCA

Two squirrels
use wild tamarind's branches
as a bridge

- CKA Linda Pauwels, MIA

19

40 leaves
fall from a branch
drowns a felled tree

-CA Glenn Mackie, DFW

We are all
a bunch
of daisies

-CA Michael Phelan, LGA

4) Vignettes Of A Pilot's Life:

This theme, by far, is the one that received the most contributions from pilots. Here, quilted together with characteristic pilot cheekiness, is a colorful patchwork of hefty things.

Schedules, hotels, weather, medical, pay, seniority, uniforms, the company, and the union. And, to close, a fitting culmination for a professional life always revolving around "what comes next."

Four o clock wake up
starbucks line is 5 miles long
damn these early flights

-FO Richard Krutenat, DFW

Too long four-day trip
My children growing quickly
Life is flying by

-FO Richard Krutenat, DFW

It's morning somewhere.
I don't know what day it is.
Where the ???? am I?

-CA Robert Sproc, DFW

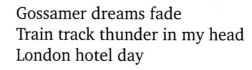

Gossamer dreams fade
Train track thunder in my head
London hotel day

-CA Carl Battis, DFW

The hotel curtains
come open just a little
every damn morning

-FO Christopher Wachter, DCA

After flying all night
steamed vegetable
gyoza

- CKA Linda Pauwels, MIA

fourteen-hour days
not really feeling
'optimized'

-CKA Linda Pauwels, MIA

Oh no! wet spot
by the front door-
uniform socks

- *CKA Linda Pauwels, MIA*

Lightning hits your plane!
Nobody will feel a thing.
You won't even flinch.

*-Shared by CA Charlotte O'Connell, MIA (career day
school visit, haiku thank you note from a 5th grader)*

Top of descent
Only thirty minutes to go
But I need to pee!

-CA Konstantin Volodzko, PHL (RET)

A list of our names
As the foliage below
Approach of Winter

-CA Bill Behymer, LAX (RET) (awaiting arbitrated seniority list integration)

I awoke in a panicked sweat...
Rushed downstairs in a fright to check...
And I was right after all,
There WAS a zero missing
From my Profit Sharing Paycheck

-CA John McIlvenna, LAX

A deal's a deal
until of course
it isn't

-CA Curtis Ladich, DFW

Roses are red
Violets are not
Gotta try to keep up
The scam is comin in hot

-FO Patrick Zeller, BOS (FUR)

Seven Seventy-seven
That I Fly High and Far
It Has Small Beds

-CA Steen Friis-Hansen, DFW (translation, originally posted in Danish)

23:15 Refrigerators
23:16 Are not something that
23:17 You need in Siberia

-CA Robert Sproc, DFW (somewhere over Russia,
haiku time-stamped on the 'Reminders' page)

"A Winter Poem"
#@!&-It's Cold
Loren – 2019

-CA Loren Banko, DCA (RET)

Chicago pre-flight
Where did summer get off to?
De-Icing Fluid!

-FO Christopher Lemon, LAX

Hernia it's not
Fixed it with a painful shot
Five more shots and done

-FO Daniel Manusos, ORD

Enjoy the new year!
It will be over too soon;
retirement looms.

-FO Carol Scherer, DFW (RET)

Mailed a box today
Ipad, ID's, keys and vest
All I can say...Best!

-CA Frank Floersh, DFW (RET)

The following haiku is an entire life as an airline pilot, reduced to three lines and a 5-7-5 format. It touched me greatly:

Thirty-eight years and
Twenty-five thousand hours.
I retired. Bye y'all.

-CA Donald Steinman, PHX (RET)

5) On Love, Hearth, and Home:

The author invited Captain Mark Cronin, former Managing Director of Line Operations at American Airlines, to write the introduction to this section.

"Love, hearth and home – to most people, these words bring feelings of warmth and comfort. As a pilot for over 30 years, these words describe a list of the things I hold most dear in life. When I became a pilot, my wife and I had two young daughters and a beloved golden retriever. I would travel for days on end, and the one thing that would get me through night after night in a mundane hotel room would be the idea of coming home to three of the biggest hugs from my daughters and my wife, a wet kiss from my dog, and a home-cooked meal. It was the little things that I began to appreciate, like a hot shower in my own bathroom and the feeling of slipping under warm covers in my own, comfortable bed.

For a career that often takes you away from love, hearth and home, it also makes you appreciate those things that much more. Over time, you find ways to hold onto the feelings those words give you when you're on the road – or I should say, in the air. The following poems are reflections from pilots who have spent time finding the balance between their love of flying and their longing for the comforts of home. I think the balance between our passion for our job and our desire to be home with our loved ones is something most pilots try to strike. I believe the best way to navigate this conundrum is to remember the age old saying – home is where the heart is."

-CA Mark Cronin, PHL

I grew up
In the Land
Of Tecumseh

-CA Michael Boring, DFW (RET) (1952-2020)

Simple yet complex
Angelical reflection
Life...a love cookie

-CA Frank Floersh, DFW (RET)

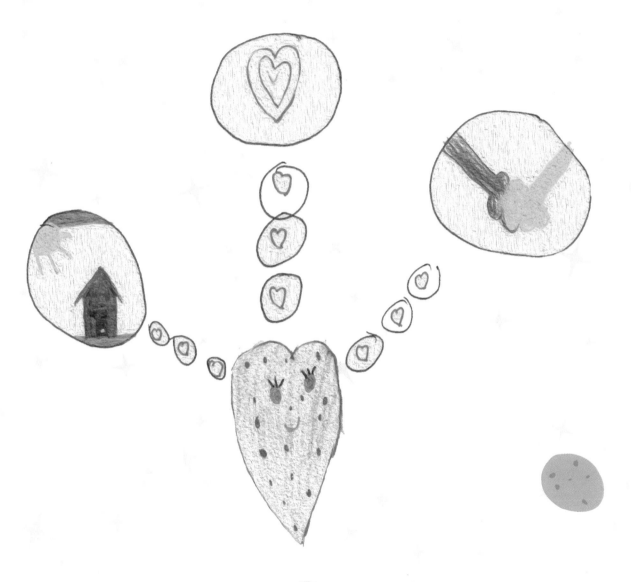

Gorgeous red Corvette
With curvy lines like her hips
The wind in her hair

-CA Michael Sigman, DFW (RET)

Labs on point, the rabbit runs
Just sit back and cradle your gun
Wait 5 min, you'll get your shot
For in circles, rabbits trot

-CA Loren Banko, DCA (RET)

It's Thanksgiving Day
Taittinger, Turkey, and Tums
The couch calls my name...

-FO Christopher Wachter, DCA

Christmas time is fun
Dreams of toys and how to play
Thank God for this day

-CA Frank Floersh, DFW (RET)

New Year's morning-
on the front porch
sweet smell of gardenia

- CKA Linda Pauwels, MIA

Light to black and black to light
A thousand reasons to ignore
A breath of soul held long and treasured
Broken hearts that will always store

-CKA Scott Christensen, DFW *(excerpt from full poem, Light)*

Bedside holding hands
His smile fades and teardrops fall
Father's light grows dim

-CA Carl Battis, DFW

Small miracles great
12 years silent might be past
his first word was "spin"

-CA David Rintel, MIA

Together one September morning
The year two thousand and one
Our day was just starting
Our lives lit up by the sun

-CA Michael Baltzer, LGA *(excerpt from poem, Angels of America)*

He said goodbye early
Too rushed to give a final hug
Not sure they heard the words
Goodbye my little Lady Bugs

Woke up with plans for later
Moving fast to beat the clock
Plans to call the house in a while
Finished the day in a box

His son became a man too early
Standing tall trying not to cry
Knowing he'd lost his hero forever
Who would teach him how to fly

-CKA Scott Christensen, DFW (excerpt from poem,
untitled)

Every wrinkle has a story
Not every one is necessarily sad
Some just come from living hard and fast
Slowing down they etch a map
From beginning to end memories are there
North and South and East and West
Remains of all the good and bad done
Sometimes failing the test

-CKA Scott Christensen, DFW (excerpt from poem,
Wrinkles and Memories)

The trail which follows the creek
up to the overlook,
where she would often linger
before turning back to hearth and home,
is a sad and lonely place now
and just as well,
for her mountain should also mourn her passing,
along with us who loved her.

-CA Konstantin Volodzko, PHL (RET)

The I Ching augured 'Danger'
But we pressed on
Flying through high wind advisories
Then winding country roads
To visit small town America
And hug our prodigal son
After a home game
Breakfast at Doris' cafe
A walk in crisp autumn air
With Gratitude for a life
Redirected

- CKA Linda Pauwels, MIA

I'm back, little house!
red front door
seems happy

- CKA Linda Pauwels, MIA

6) On Continuity:

The poems in this section were composed by pilots undergoing flight training through the American Airlines Cadet Academy. Their words serve to symbolically integrate a future generation of fliers into our fold.

"Children," I say plainly, "watch out for the baobabs!"[4]

God told me to fly
Up to the mountain sky high
We will land in 5

-Keith Taylor, Asst. Chief Pilot, Coast Flight, Dallas, TX

Flying, freedom, wings
Loved ones from across the world
Beauty connection

-Kristin Sito, CTI, Millingon, TN

8 pm
Jeppesen and noodles again
Clear Prop!

-Jordan Carty, Coast Flight, Dallas, TX

---

[4]Saint-Exupéry, *The Little Prince*, 74.

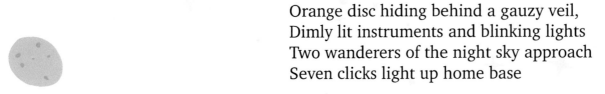

Orange disc hiding behind a gauzy veil,
Dimly lit instruments and blinking lights
Two wanderers of the night sky approach
Seven clicks light up home base

-Nathalie Pauwels, CTI, Millington, TN

AFTERWORD

The initial draft of this book was sent to the publisher on October 1, 2020, the day American Airlines began furloughing the first wave of 1605 pilots. As of this writing, the worldwide airline industry remains deeply affected by COVID-19, and our future is uncertain.

It's a good thing pilots know how to operate when best laid plans don't go as expected! In measures large and small, that's often how it turns out when we strap in to go flying. We will continue to rely on rules, procedures, and threat and error models to ensure we fly safely. The glue that ties everything together, however, is the accumulated experience of the pilots at the controls, embodying the lessons of those who came before us.

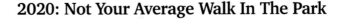

2020: Not Your Average Walk In The Park

The smart phone announces, tinnily:
"8 minutes to Andrew Brown Park"
where a walk in cool morning air
brings respite from the north Texas heat.
What shade of blue is the sky today?
Cyan, I swiftly conclude
as my mind's eye brings forth
this particular hue,
common to route two
on the nav display.
Is there any beauty to be found
among the concrete sinews
we call modern pathways?
The answer comes in contrasts:
A great blue heron takes flight
staying in ground effect over the lake,
to a perfect landing on the other side.
One graceful ancient flier- oblivious
to the moving shadow cast
by a half-filled airliner
on short final
overhead.

-*CKA Linda Pauwels, MIA*

POSTSCRIPT

"I am the one. I bring spring to the azaleas, I bring the sun."[5]

CA Chuck Tripi, LGA (RET) from poem White Azaleas

---

[5] Chuck Tripi, "White Azaleas" in Killer *Pavement Ahead*, (Allahabad, India: Cyberwit.net, 2015), 13.

BIBLIOGRAPHY

Beilenson, Peter, ed., *Japanese Haiku*. New York: Peter Pauper, 1955. www.sacred-texts.com.

Saint-Exupéry, Antoine de. *The Little Prince*. New York: Harcourt Brace & Company, 1943.

Tripi, Chuck. "White Azaleas" in *Killer Pavement Ahead*. Allahabad, India: Cyberwit.net, 2015.

Contributing Authors (Pilots)

CA Michael Baltzer
CA Loren Banko
CA Carl Battis
CA Bill Behymer
CA Michael Boring
CKA Scott Christensen
CA Mark Cronin
CA John Drindak
CA Frank Floersh
CA Steen Friis-Hansen
FO Timothy Hamel
CA Thomas Hill
CKA Gregory Hudson
CA Ronald Hunt
FO Richard Krutenat
CA Curtis Ladich
CA Gerardo Lami
FO Christopher Lemon
CA Glenn Mackie
FO Daniel Manusos
CA John McIlvenna
FO Roger Mortensen
CA Charlotte O'Connell
CA Michael Phelan
CA David Rintel
FO Carol Scherer
CA Michael Sigman
CA Robert Sproc
CA Donald Steinman
CA Mark Treider
CA Konstantin Volodzko
FO Christopher Wachter
CKA Wendy Young
FO Patrick Zeller

AA Cadet Academy Pilots

Jordan Carty
Nathalie Pauwels
Kristin Sito
Keith Taylor

Illustration Credits

Cover: Joseph Govin, age 10 (airplane) and Scarlett O'Malley, age 12 (planet and rose)
Cover Design: Manuel Serna, Cover Concept: Linda Pauwels

Kinley Johnson, age 12, page 4
Sophia Downard, age 15, page 5
Davis Kwasny, age 11, page 13
Selah Coy, age 8, page 15
Fiona Pfeiffer, age 10, page 17
Char Young, age 13, page 18
Rebecca Peitz, age 15, page 19
Monica Kwasny, age 9, page 20

-Daisy collage, from left to right, rows top to bottom: page 22

Scarlett O'Malley, Kaylee Burkitt, Rebecca Peitz, Penelope Neilon
Joseph Govin, Jacob Govin, Sophia Downard, Selah Coy
Jacqueline Ruiz, Fiona Pfeiffer, Davis Kwasny, Skye Stauffer
Sam Young, Callista Chabot, Giullianna Ruiz (age 11), Nathalie Pauwels

Kaylee Burkitt, age 8, page 25
Jacob Govin, age 10, page 26
Sam Young, age 13, page 28
Callista Chabot, age 17, page 32
Penelope Neilon, age 6, page 33
Callista Chabot, age 17, page 35
LT Nathalie Pauwels, USN (age 9 on 9/11), page 37
Ella Claire Basset, age 10, page 40
Sophia Downard, age 15, page 42
Skye Stauffer, age 15, page 43

ABOUT THE AUTHOR

Captain Linda Pauwels is an airline pilot. For over three decades she has flown thousands of hours, on many types of big airplanes, all over the world. Linda even counts some aviation "firsts" attached to her name. At present, she instructs and evaluates pilots as a check airman on the Boeing 787 for American Airlines.

Linda was born in San Pedro, Buenos Aires, Argentina. She came to the United States at age six, after the death of her father. Having experienced adversity early on in life, she grew to understand and appreciate the value of resilience. Linda integrates intuition and sensitivity, along with a graduate academic preparation in education, in her professional life.

In the mid-2000s, Linda wrote a regular column, titled From the Cockpit, for the Orange County Register. She has been secretly writing poetry for a while. Unfortunately, that cat is now out of the bag.

Linda has been married to Frederick, also a pilot, for almost forty years. They have two adult children, Nathalie and Patrick, domestic animals, and an Asian garden with a bird feeder. The family has a primary base in North Texas, near DFW airport and a secondary base in South Florida, near MIA.

Coming Soon:

Beyond Haiku: Women Pilots Write Poetry

Made in the USA
Las Vegas, NV
12 December 2021